HARRY HILL'S BUMPER BOOK OF BLOOPERS

HARRY HILL'S

BUMPER BOOK OF BLOOPERS

ff

faber and faber

First published in 2011
by Faber and Faber Limited
Bloomsbury House, 74–77 Great Russell Street,
London WC1B 3DA

Printed in the UK by CPI Group (UK) Ltd, Croydon, CR0 4YY
Design by Faber and Faber Ltd

A CIP record for this book
is available from the British Library

ISBN 978-0-571-28174-9

2 4 6 8 10 9 7 5 3 1

Dear Raiders,

Thinks for bullying this new booze of burpers.
Who a minks dust can honestly slave wee hove
Najaf made a moustache when rating an antwerp or
some usher peace of prozac?

Ofcom horse these daze with the Ben Hur fit of con
pewters it is passable to fax most herons with
the sample clique of a bourbon using slush pearl
jams as smell cheque. Howl funghi it is though to
reed sumo these mouse prints! I butter the feeble
hoover maid them felt lick right Charlenes weiner
they red thumb back. I have a trumpet to organ eyes
the varicose bluberries into cattle gorys such as
animos, Seal liberties, Loaf and mad ridge, spots,
and grime and spanish mint. Father we have pushed
them in alfafa betty nautical ordeuvres.

If yew marriage two spots any bupa in snooze
papers or margarines or heathen an ad virgin
mental in a ship widow I wood arc ewe to police
pose them hear to meat at the pebble dashers
Fibber and Fazer.

I hop you engine oil the burka,
Yours since early,

Hairy Hell

P.S. Ed could you chick spooling for me? Ta, H

HARRY HILL'S BLOOPERS

It does not help if the book is full
if misprints and spelling mistakes.

The Spectator

Animals

Widow in bed with a case of salmon, city court told

Liverpool Echo

A Portsmouth man believes he has found the way to talk to hedgehogs – although he does not know the meaning of what he says to them.

Evening News

A monkey trained to pick coconuts jumped on to a man passing a coconut tree in Kuala Lumpur. He mistook his head for a nut and tried to twist it off. The man was taken to hospital with a strained neck.

Sunday Mirror

I don't understand how the confusion arose!

Late that same evening, after a vain search all round the village, Mary found the dog dead in the garden. She curried the body indoors.

Short story

In many parts of Co. Sligo hares are now practically unknown because of the unreasonable laughter to which they have been subjected in recent years.

Sligo paper

Said Mr Justice Vaisey: 'It is a fearful thing to contemplate that, when you are driving along the road, a heavy horse may at any moment drop from the sky on top of you.'

Daily Graphic

The Tasmanian wolf is striped like a tiger, has a tail like a rat, is a relative of opossums, and is the youngest man ever to be president of the United States.

The Telegram (Bridgewater, Connecticut)

CATTLE PLEASE CLOSE GATE

Notice at Gloucester farm

The Game Commission of Pennsylvania has made a thorough review of the mammas of Pennsylvania and finds that there are more than fifty species.

Clarion Democrat, Pennsylvania

Icelandic fish talks– not likely

Grimsby Telegraph

The new lizard, 21 in. long, is said at the Zoo to be settling down well. It is described by a keeper as being as lively as the cricketers that are part of its favourite diet.

Lincolnshire Echo

ARCHAEOLOGISTS ATTACK DEAD ELEPHANT

Athens News

At a lunch hour assembly at the school, Mrs Thomson gave an interesting talk, with slides, on Baboo, her pet baboon. She said that, although some people were scared by such a large animal, she felt completely at home with him, having spent fifteen years in Africa with her husband.

School newsletter

Birth and Death

No comment!

After viewing the headless, armless, and legless torso, Coroner Marvin Rogers and Coast Guard Captain Willie E. Carr both voiced the opinion that the 65-year-old real estate agent had been slain.

Philadelphia Inquirer

PERSONS ARE PROHIBITED FROM PICKING FLOWERS FROM ANY BUT THEIR OWN GRAVES

Sign in cemetery

Homicide victims rarely talk to police

Express-Times

This year marks the thirtieth anniversary of the death of Sergei M. Eisenstein, as well as the eighteenth anniversary of his birth.

BFI News

John Wilson had suffered from attacks of pneumonia and jaundice but, at Linton Hospital, near Maidstone, he died from arterial sclerosis.

'It will be a miracle if he ever paints again,' said his wife Barbara.

Sevenoaks Chronicle

POLICE in Hawick yesterday called off a search for a 20-year-old man who is believed to have frowned after falling into the swollen River Teviot.

Scotsman

She has visited the cemetery where her husband was buried on a number of occasions.

Shropshire Star

g...ns are

IN MEMORIAM
In loving memory of a
very dead Dad, who
died April 20th, 1956.

their own

In last week's issue some errors were made regarding Mrs Gilcuddy, which the following account will correct: Mrs Gilcuddy was born in 1865, and was 64 years and 11 days of age at the time of her birth.

Santa Ana Record, California

FATHER OF TEN SHOT DEAD
Mistaken for rabbit

Headline in New York paper

Due to an error in transmission we stated in an inquest report on Saturday that Mrs Susannah Vincent, of Porth, was found dead with a bottle in her left hand and a plastic bag over her head. This should have read 'a Bible in her left hand'. We apologise for any distress caused to the family.

Swindon Evening Advertiser

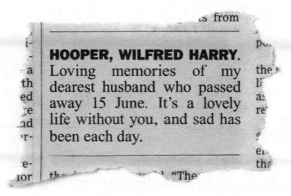

HOOPER, WILFRED HARRY.
Loving memories of my
dearest husband who passed
away 15 June. It's a lovely
life without you, and sad has
been each day.

Northants Evening Telegraph

31

et
d

Auctioneer Finds Body In Funeral Home

Remains of 12 others left in closed business

selcebrityies

'Beyond its entertainment value, Baywatch has enriched and, in so many cases, helped save lives.'

David Hasselhoff

Hi I'm The Hoff

'I love being in America.'

Charlotte Church, while visiting Toronto

'I get to lots of
overseas places, like Canada.'

US-based Britney Spears

'I've never really wanted to go to Japan. Simply because I don't like eating fish. And I know that's very popular out there in Africa.'

Britney Spears

'I've got taste. It's inbred in me.'

David Hasselhoff

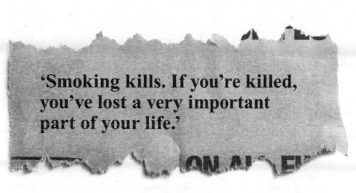

'Smoking kills. If you're killed, you've lost a very important part of your life.'

Brooke Shields

'So, where's the Cannes Film
Festival being held this year?'

Christina Aguilera

'I've been noticing gravity since
I was very young.'

Cameron Diaz

'I don't know much
about football.
I know what a goal
is, which is surely
the main thing
about football.'

Victoria Beckham

'I live my life day by day, and that's how I continue to live it.'

Naomi Campbell

'Doesn't that hurt?'

Anna Nicole Smith on suicide bombers

'We have a lot of kids who don't know what work means. They think work is a four-letter word.'

Hillary Clinton

'The Union Jack is for all of us, but the
St George is just for London, isn't it?'

Jade Goody

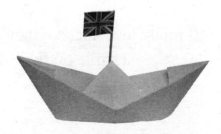

'I really love ducks – they've always got
a smile on their face.'

Richard Madeley

'Fiction writing is great. You can make up almost anything.'

Ivana Trump, on completing her first novel

'So Carol, you're a housewife and mother. And have you got any children?'

Michael Barrymore

Crime and Punishment

The police arrested two IRA leaders, David O'Connell and Joe O'Neill, after an IRA funeral later today, but that appeared to be connected to a souffle during the funeral.

International Herald Tribune

A man stole the TV while the occupants of the house were watching it, a court heard. The 42-year-old man calmly unplugged the set, told the occupants he was taking it for 'forensic' and left.

Staffordshire Evening Sentinel

By an unfortunate typographical error we were made to say last week that the retiring Mr —— was a member of the defective branch of the police force. Of course this should have read: 'The detective branch of the police farce.'

New Zealand paper

FEDERAL AGENTS RAID GUN SHOP, FIND WEAPONS

When Miss Virginia Brenholtz, 17, of 911 Franklin Avenue, awakened to find a burglar at her bedside early Sunday, she gave him a shave and screamed for help.

Columbus Citizen, Ohio

After being woken from a drunken

sleep and asked to leave the home of

his wife, a 41-year-old labourer became

violet and struck out.

Rhyl Journal and Advertiser

A week after a brick had hurtled through a shop window in Grange Mount causing £64 of damage, a 19-year-old youth returned to the shop and asked for his brick back. He then complained to a police officer that the shopkeeper would not return it, said Inspector Cole, prosecuting.

Birkenhead News

Two Convicts Evade Noose: Jury Hung

A bottle of whisky and a bottle of sherry were stolen by a gurglar who forced a window of a house in Granfield Avenue, Radcliffe-on-Trent, last night.

Nottingham Evening Post and Standard

We have been unable to publish a letter on vandalism from Mrs Elizabeth Stewart of Oak Road, Abronhill. It arrived badly charred after vandals set fire to a letterbox in Abronhill.

Cumbernauld News

There were 26 people there, 22 men and four women, drinking beer and spirits. Four full 11-gallon canisters of beer, five empty ones, one part full, 415 cans of pale ale and lager, 22 partly full cans, 68 empty cans, and several dozen beer and spirit glasses were found.

'I came to the conclusion that this was a place used for drinking,' said the inspector.

Scotsman

Collene Campbell Champions the Rights of Murder Victims After Being One Herself More Than Once

Grange County Register, California

When Frank Rea, a club entertainer who astonished audiences as 'The Amazing Memoranda', was asked by a social security officer how much work he did on the side, he said he did not remember.

Altrincham Guardian

Police investigating a break-in at the home of Norman Fowler MP had no difficulty in identifying the culprit, magistrates heard last Thursday. One of the three burglars, a 19-year-old Irishman, left his birth certificate behind.

Sutton Coldfield News

Police chased the getaway cat for more than 40 miles.

Daily Mail

P.G. Police Say Detective Shot Man With Knife

Washington Post

Detective Constable Patricia Basely (30) said today she was 'a very lucky woman' after being hit by the car, carried ten yards on the bonnet and then having her leg run over.

Northampton Chronicle and Echo

Robert Leys, a taxi driver who wears an SS cap and long boots, dresses in black and entertains his passengers with tapes of Nazi party war songs, has had his licence to drive a taxi revoked. Mr Leys said he would fight any attempt to take away his licence. 'This is the sort of thing that happened in Nazi Germany,' he said.

Sydney Herald

Legislator Wants Tougher Death Penalty

Irish police are being handicapped in a search for a stolen van, because they cannot issue a description. It's a special branch vehicle, and they don't want the public to know what it looks like.

Guardian

Drunk Gets Nine Months In Violin Case

Constable John Knight told the Court that on 30 June David Durbin had said to him: 'I'll kill you.' 'Did he kill you?' asked the prosecutor, Mr H. A. Kelly.

Rand Daily Mail

A VISUALLY IMPAIRED San Francisco man argued he wasn't driving solo in the commuter lane reserved for cars carrying two or more people because his dog, Queenie, was helping him navigate.

Seattle Times

Doctors and Hospitals

Looks like Plague

DOCTOR

It wasn't the proper doctor –
just a young locust taking his
place while he was away.

Short story in The Evening New

REAL BONE HALF-SKELETON, in better condition than seller. £250.

British Medical Journal

The seaman, severely injured when the ship was three hours out, was taken to hospital and the hippopotamus removed.

Daily Telegraph

A TRANSPLANT SURGEON has called for a ban on 'kidneys-for-ale' operations.

Daily Mail

Putting urine in your ears not recommended to treat sinus infection

The many friends of Mrs Barrett will be sorry to learn that she injured her foot on Saturday. It will probably be six weeks before the fool can be released from a plaster cast.

Toronto newspaper

**One man was admitted to hospital
suffering from buns.**

Bristol paper

HEALTH OFFICIALS: POOLS, DIARRHEA NOT GOOD MIX

World Herald

American research, which is gaining support in Britain, shows that problem drinkers have recognisable habits, gulping or taking large sips of their drinks, and rarely putting their lasses down.

Guardian

I recommend my patients to eat
the tables with their meat, and
to be careful not to swallow their
food too quickly·

Medical Weekly

Females likelier to test for women's diseases

Associated Press

Mr Ross's flab-fighting efforts, which reduced his 15-stone frame to two stone, won himself a buffet banquet for 80 and a portable colour television.

Harrogate Advertiser

MEDICAL EXAM ANSWERS

The skeleton is what is left after the insides have been taken out and the outsides have been taken off. The purpose of the skeleton is something to hitch meat on.

The three kinds of blood vessels are arteries, veins and caterpillars.

The alimentary canal is located in the northern part of Alabama.

To remove dust from the eye: pull the eye down over the nose.

For nosebleeds, put the nose lower than the body until the heart stops.

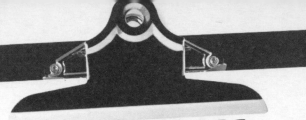

By the time he was admitted, his rapid heart had stopped, and he was feeling better.

On the second day the knee was better and on the third day it had completely disappeared.

The patient has no past history of
suicides.

Patient has left his white blood
cells at another hospital.

Patient's fluid intake is good,
mostly beer.

She slipped on the ice and
apparently her legs went in
separate directions in early
December.

The patient left the hospital
feeling much better except for her
original complaints.

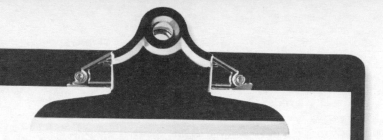

The patient refused an autopsy.

Discharge status: alive but without permission.

She is numb from her toes down.

Family

On the same bus as myself was a schoolboy whose head had become stuck in a vase. His mother was rushing him off to hospital. Presumably to avoid attracting attention she had placed her son's school cap on top of the vase.

Letter in John Bull, quoted in New Statesman

CHILDREN of A Rawashid area in Abu Dhabi will be inoculated against polio, mums and whooping cough as from next Tuesday.

Khaleej Times

'I was with Ian while he was at the club. He is not uncontrollable. He is big, but then boys are bigger than girls. None of the other mothers complained to me. Ian did shut Mrs Carter's little girl in a trunk. He's a naturally tidy child and puts all things away.'

Birmingham Post

He and his wife Gillian, who is a teacher, have three children, Gaven aged 13 and 11-year-old twins ugh and Helen.

Orpington News Shopper

Mrs Blackhouse, 37, and her two children, Harry, 10, and Sophie, 77, were on holiday last night.

Daily Express

**Keeping all food under cover
is the first step towards ridding
the house of aunts.**

Albany Journal

Children shot for Christmas in the home – Regent Photographic Studios.

Morecambe Visitor

I am forwarding my marriage certificate and my 3 children, one of which was a mistake as you can see.

Letter to local government agency

In accordance with your instructions,
I have given birth to twins in the
enclosed envelope

State Population To Double By 2040; Babies To Blame

McClatchy News Service

Food and Drink

AS FROM MONDAY,
THE CATERING ASSISTANTS
WILL SERVE CUSTOMERS
TO ALL POTATOES

Factory noticeboard

Order chicken cut into serving pieces. Clean as necessary. Wash, drain, and blot on absorbent paper. Place chicken in deep bowl. Mash in a mortar the garlic, oregano, salt and peppercorns. Add to rum, mixed with soy sauce. Pour over children.

Ridgewood Record, New Jersey

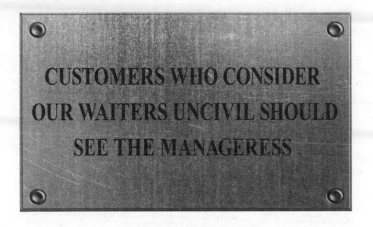

Sign in restaurant

Birds Eye recently gave a banquet at which the Minister of Housing was guest of honor pre-cooked, frozen and re-heated on site.

Catering Management

BLOOPER MENU

Lovely Assmosphere
We use over 50 species in our cooking

❧

ENTRIES

Shrotted imps
Consomme with poodles
Smoked Solomon
Uncared Ham
Mule's Marinère

❧

MAIN CURSES

Veal in Breadcrumbs Friend in Butter

Quick Lorraine
Stir-fried garbage
Human Chicken (Chinese)
Tuna and sweatcorn
Chicken Cordon Blow
Steamed dumpings
Grilled chicken breath

Sweat and Sour Chicken
Braised Kids with Pee
Turkey Breast in Butt
Mixed girrl and baked beings
Kidneys of the Chef
Caramelized Opinions
Thousand Ireland dressing

❧

DESERTS

Turdy Delight
Sweat from the trolley
Pancakes with pure male syrup
Chocolate Puke
Roguefart cheese
Coffee and mice pies

I always scatter crumbs on the waiter to attract the fish.

Angler's Mail

Mai Thai Finn is one of the students in the program and was in the center of the photo. We incorrectly listed her name as one of the items on the menu.

Community Life

**DINE HERE –
ALLAH CART**

Sign in Pakistan restaurant

For coping with unexpected guests, it is always a good plan to keep a few tons of sardines in the house.

Woman's Weekly

**PLEASE CHECK
THE NEXT FREEZER FOR
BOOGERS, FRIES, PIZZA &
ALL BREAKFAST
PRODUCTS**

Costright, Turks and Calcos Islands

Washington (Reuters) – Quaker Maid Meats Inc. on Tuesday said it would voluntarily recall 94,400 pounds of frozen ground beef panties that may be contaminated with E. coli.

New York Times website

When you next have friends to dinner, one cut up in a mixed salad would be plenty for eight and a novel surprise for one's guests.

Woman's Weekly

New Group Product Manager at KP Foods is John Koster, previously with Kentucky Fried Children. Mr Koster joins the KP Nuts team . . .

Supermarketing

If water contains sediment,
let it stand, then strain through
a clean muslim.

Hereford Times

INSTRUCTIONS: OPEN PACKET, EAT NUTS

On an American Airlines pack of nuts

SERVING SUGGESTION: DEFROST

On Swann frozen meals

FOR HEAT-RETAINING CORRUGATED
CARDBOARD TECHNOLOGY TO
FUNCTION PROPERLY, CLOSE LID

Instruction on Domino's pizza box

Pasta Salad mixed with either chunks of fish or baby, barely cooked broad beans, then dressed with oil and vinegar, is very good, too.

Irish Times

Geography

Dear Tourist,

Welcome to Jordan, the Holy Land, the loud of freasures and pleasures. We present to you this 'Touvist Guide' to help facilitate your stoy and we are glad to tell you how happy we are in your prescence.

Jordan This Week

Absent-minded Ray and Joyce Elkeron had a great time on a day trip – but haven't got a clue where they went! Now they have put an ad in the paper asking people if they recognise their description of the beauty spot.

It was only after they got home and planned a return trip that they realised they had no idea where they had been.

The Sun

'On my first day of Junior High I was in Geography class, and the teacher asked us if anybody knew the names of the continents. And I was sooo excited. I was like, Dammit! It's my first day of 7th grade, I'm in Junior High and I know this answer. So I raised my hand, I was the first one, and I said A-E-I-O-U!'

Jessica Simpson

GEOGRAPHY HOMEWORK

A fjord is a Norwegian car.

Soviet is another name for a table napkin.

The Sewage Canal is in Egypt.

Tarzan is a short name for the American flag. The full name is Tarzan Stripes.

Tunisia is a disease where you lose your memory.

The people who live in Paris are called Parisites.

The North Pole is so cold that the people who live there have to live somewhere else.

The Easter game of egg rolling started in Debenhams and Cornwall.

Elf and safety

It's a good idea, before you give your hair its nightly brushing, to begin the operation with a brick massage to loosen your scalp and to start the circulation of the blood.

Ann Arbor News, Michigan

The first essential in the treatment of burns is that the patient should be removed from the fire.

First Aid Manual

Mr S. Butters for reasons of ill health, is permanently discontinuing widow cleaning.

Cambridgeshire Times

Arthur Kitchener was seriously burned Saturday afternoon when he came in contact with a high voltage wife.

Surrey Advertiser

DANGER!

TO TOUCH THESE WIRES WILL RESULT IN INSTANT DEATH. ANYONE FOUND DOING SO WILL BE SEVERELY PROSECUTED.

Sign on electricity pylon

In the interests of hygiene,
please use tongues when
picking up your baked potatoes

Sign in canteen, BBC Manchester

Experts: Fewer Blows To Head Would Reduce Brain Damage

News and Observer (Raleigh, North Carolina)

SOME USEFUL INSTRUCTIONS

On a Sainsbury's peanut packet

PRODUCT WILL BE HOT AFTER HEATING

Label on a Marks and Spencer bread pudding

DO NOT IRON CLOTHES ON BODY

Instruction on a Rowenta iron

DO NOT USE WHILE SLEEPING

Instruction on a Sears hairdryer

DO NOT TURN UPSIDE DOWN

Instruction on bottom of a Tesco tiramisu box

WEARING OF THIS GARMENT DOES NOT ENABLE YOU TO FLY

Warning on child's Superman costume

DO NOT DRIVE
CAR OR OPERATE
MACHINERY

Label on Boots children's cough medicine

History

Anne Berlin

As Hannibal urged his 40,000 men and 37 elephants across the Alps in 218 BC, he could have had little idea that he would be followed 2,200 years later by a party of 20 boys and four masters from Oswestry School, among them 14-year-old Stephen Jones, from Bulford Camp.

Salisbury Journal

The extinction may well have occurred when a steroid hit the Earth.

Sunday Times

Britain protected the Hugenots
persecuted by Louise XIV.

Guardian

The skeleton was believed to be that of a Saxon worrier.

Express and Echo

Henry VIII by his own efforts increased
the population of England by 40,000.

Northern San Diego Shopper's Guide

'The Holocaust was an obscene period in our nation's history. I mean in this century's history. But we all lived in this century. I didn't live in this century.'

Dan Quayle, former US Vice-President

HISTORY HOMEWORK

The second wife of Henry VIII was Ann Berlin.

Socrates died from an overdose of wedlock.

Sir Walter Raleigh circumcised the world with a big clipper.

In the field near our house they think they have discovered the remains of a Roman fart.

Home

Nothing brightens the garden in spring more than primrose pants.

Weekly paper

DOVER ROAD

Semi-det. house with sea through lounge.

Folkestone, Hythe and District Herald

A spacious 3 bed semi-detached property comprising 3 god sized bedrooms and a large loving room.

Leamington Spa Courier

WOMAN WANTED, to share Fat with another.

MALE (24) seeks doom in central flat.
Please phone . . .

Edinburgh Evening News

Peaceful, relaxing, self-contained, stone built cottages and bungalows. Sandy beach only 300 years away.

Wales Holidays 1983 brochure

... a substantial well-built semi ...
3 bedrooms ... garden areas to front
and rear with fish pong.

Stockport Express

A detached 213 bedroom
bungalow on large corner plot.

South Wales Echo

FOR RENT: 6-room hated apartment.

FOR SALE:
A rarely comfortable
modern detached
residence.

Irish Times

International News

Here is the Newt

He had the privilege also of viewing
a number of rare Egyptian tummies.

Cleveland (Ohio) paper

Two Fast Germans escaped to West Berlin during the night in the second escape this week, police said yesterday.

Hong Kong Standard

Every commissioned officer is promoted directly from the ranks – there's nothing except sheer ability to stop you achieving a high position in the New Zealand armed forces.

Auckland Star

The Reserve Bank, which manages the rand' sexchange rate, has apparently decided to call a halt to its slide.

Financial Times

At the same time, however, it was
clear that both sides wished to avoid
a direct navel confrontation in the
Gulf of Tongking.

Sunday Telegraph

Scandinavia has no doubt that in the latter
half of last week a naval engagement took
place between Great Britain and Germany
in the North Sea. The evidence is that of
kippers who, using their eyes and ears, put
two and two together.

The Star

Solar System Expected
To Be Back In Operation

Libertyville Herald

Quarter Of A Million Chinese Live On Water

WASHINGTON – On orders from the White Mouse, the FBI last night sealed off the offices of the ousted special Watergate prosecutor Archibald Cox and his staff.

International Herald Tribune

Army vehicle disappears

An Australian Army vehicle worth $74,000 has gone missing after being painted with camouflage.

Iraqi head seeks arms

Jobs

I could
Moo-der
a pint!

WANTED – Man to take care of cow that does not smoke or drink.

Pickens Sentinel

I would like to be an accountant but you have to know a lot about moths.

From a school essay

3-year old teacher needed for pre-school. Experience preferred.

WANTED – Gardener; must be experienced, or useless.

Advert in Wiltshire paper

CV BLOOPERS

Career break in 1999 to renovate my horse.

Enjoy cooking Chinese and Italians.

2001 summer –
Voluntary work for taking care of the elderly and vegetable people.

Reason for leaving last job:
Maturity leave

Job Duties: Answer phones, file papers, respond to customer e-mails, take odors.

Qualifications: Twin sister has accounting degree.

Languages:
Speak English and Spinach.

pardon?

I am about to enrol on a Business and Finance Degree with the Open University. I feel that this qualification will prove detrimental to me for future success.

Strengths: Ability
to meet deadlines
while maintaining
composer.

Work experience: Maintained files and reports, did data processing, cashed employees' paychecks.

Here are my qualifications for you to overlook.

Instrumental in ruining entire operation for a Midwest chain store.

I'm a rabid typist.

I demand a salary comiserate with my extensive experience.

Languages: French with a dictionary.
I speak fluently English.

Worked in a consulting office where I carried out my own accountant.

Personal Profile: A Netherlandphile with two grown children, a cat who snores, a Labrador with eczema and a passion for perfection.

Letters

Dear Sir,

With reference to our letter re Majorca tour, the flight you mention is completely booked, but we will inform you immediately someone falls out, as usually happens.

Letter from travel agent

The best thing to do with people who write anonymous letters is to put them straight in the fire.

Letter in provincial paper

He gets every anonymous letter that is sent in and sees to it that the writers are answered.

New York Times

When my husband reads in bed on warm nights he puts a colander over his head. He says it keeps off flies, shades his eyes from the light and lets in air at the same time – *Mrs L. Taylor, Bradford.*

Letter in Good Shopping

Dear Madam,

With reference to your blue raincoat, our manufacturers have given the garment in question a thorough testing, and find that it is absolutely waterproof. If you will wear it on a dry day, and then take it off and examine it you will see that our statement is correct.

Your obedient servants,
Bank & Co, Drapers

Local News

A SMOCK

NO SMOCKING

In the handicrafts exhibition at Wordsley Community Centre, the contribution of the Misses Smith was 'smocking and rugs' and not 'smoking drugs' as stated in last week's report.

County Express (Stourbridge)

Chip shop owner battered man

Gateshead Post

A Socialist Centre spokesman said the phone call was made by a man with a slight Scottish accident.

Newcastle Evening Chronicle

A £50,000 plus research project aimed at establishing the best means of subtitling TV programmes for deaf and partially-dead people is to be carried out at Southampton University.

Southern Evening Echo

Oxford City Council is to press the Thames Water Authority to help improve sanity facilities along the river banks running through the city.

Oxford Times

A plague to commemorate the transfer of the fund is now on display at the HCBA's old people's home at Wimbledon.

Journal of the Hotel, Catering and International Management Association

a 30 foot
Laddy

4 foot shorts

Firemen had to rescue a 15-year-old
Bramsholce boy who got stuck up a tree last
night. They had to use a 30ft laddy before
they could get Andrew Brown down.

Hull Daily Mail

This is Santa's first visit to Edlington and weather permitting, he will tour the streets of Edlington to arrive at his ghetto at S&N's at 2pm on Saturday 26th.

Doncaster Advertiser

In the Doncaster district, there are more underground cables than overhead, but this is largely due to Doncaster having its cables underground.

Yorkshire Evening Post

Traffic tailed back as far as Hemel Hempstead from the contra-flow system near the Berry Grove junction at Bushey where a bride is being re-painted at night and during the weekends.

Luton Evening Post-Echo

For the flypast, four fighter jets blazed through the sky accompanied by the RAF Innsworth band.

The Citizen, Gloucester

In a recent report of a competition held at one of Pontin's holiday camps it was inadvertently stated that it was for 'elephant' grandmothers instead of elegant grandmothers. We apologise to Mrs Helen P––, who gained third place, for any embarrassment this may have caused.

Stockport Advertiser

During the interval the huge park was full of the local gentry that arrived in hundreds of cars and ate excellent home-made cakes under an enormous marquise.

Manchester Evening News

Gerald Harris, whose name was incorrectly given as Harold Morris and who is 39 and not 93 as stated in the story, is an associate professor of Tort Law School and not a janitor at the public library as the story incorrectly stated.

Dalhousie Gazette

The evening of Clairvoyance on Tuesday 4th December at 7 p.m. has been cancelled owing to unforeseen circumstances.

Notice in East Kent Times

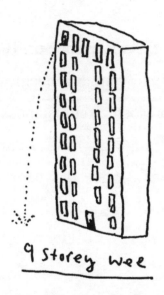

9 storey wee

'It makes me want to wee, when I hear that we are getting a new nine-storey office block on the site of the old Golden Eagle pub in Hill Street,' he said.

Birmingham Evening Mail

Commenting on a complaint from a Mr Arthur Purdey about a large gas bill, a spokesman for North West Gas said: 'We agree it was rather high for the time of year. It's possible Mr Purdey has been charged for the gas used up during the explosion that blew his house to pieces.'

Bangkok Post

Sign at Victoria Station

Missippi's literacy program shows improvement

Associated Press

Cynthia Bertross, the celebrated soprano, was involved in a serious road accident last month. We are happy to report that she was able to appear this evening in four pieces.

Worthing Gazette

A YOUNG GIRL who was blown out to sea on a set of inflatable teeth was rescued by a man on an Inflatable lobster. A coastguard spokesman commented, 'This sort of thing is all too common.'

The Times

Red Tape Holds Up New Bridge

Milford Citizen

Love

~~Luv~~ and Marij _{riage}
     ᶺ   ᶺ

Municipal Judge Charles S. Peery, who performed the brief wedding ceremony, said plaintively: 'I forgot to kill the bride. And I'm sorry.'

Tarrytown News

Close look at dating finds men choose attractive women

The Associated Press

The three-tiered wedding cage had been
made by the bride.

Somerset County Gazette

MR AND MRS SIMON PETERS
REQUEST THE HONOUR OF YOUR PRESENTS
AT THE MARRIAGE OF THEIR DAUGHTERS
EVE
TO
MR JAMES JOHNSON

For what lad can behold a pretty girl weeping for him without drying her ears on his breast.

Boston Globe

The bridesmaid wore a dress in the same material as that of the bridge.

Shropshire Journal

Bride Of Two Mouths Sues Husband

**WEDDING DRESS
FOR SALE**

Worn once, by mistake

Best man was the bridegroom's brother, Mr Martin Gasson. A reception was held at Langford's Hotel, Hove, and the couple are honeymooning in grease.

Shoreham Herald

She went on, 'I guess our marriage was beginning to disintegrate about a year and a half before we parted. A lot of it had to do with a midwife crisis because George was not working at the time . . .'

Manchester Evening News

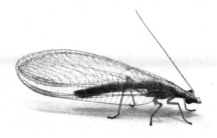

The bride wore a gown of sheer white lace with lace insects.

Cleveland newspaper

Politics

A clenched Fish

Then one of the newer Labour MPs rushed across the floor to shake a clenched fish in the Prime Minister's face.

Western Mail, Cardiff

Ford, Reagan Neck in Presidential Primary

Ethiopian Herald

'What's my view on drugs? I've forgotten my view on drugs.'

Boris Johnson

An immigrant could be rejected for any of a dozen reasons – communicable disease, illiteracy, no visible means of support or the very suspicion of immortality.

Journey to America video, PBS, 1990

'That's just the tip of the ice cube'

Ex-MP Neil Hamilton

The strike leaders had called a meeting that was to have been held in a bra near the factory, but it was too small to hold them all.

South London Press

252

Miner strike ballet to go ahead

ON A...

'I have opinions of my own –
strong opinions – but I don't
always agree with them.'

George W. Bush

Picketing miners
who have stood
round the clock at
one Yorkshire power
station have now withdrawn
their guard. The men braved
this week's cold and rain
outside Halifax's power station
until a kindly policeman told
them the truth: the power station closed
down three years ago.

Yorkshire Post

Basil Brush M.P.

When the vote was called for on a show of hands Mr Newcombe announced: 'That looks pretty unanimous for strike action.' His words were drowned by a roar of protest. There were repeated shouts of 'rubbish!' and 'it's a fox!'

The Times

Religion

SICK BOWL
(Please give Generously)

Would the congregation please note that the bowl at the back of the church labelled 'for the sick' is for monetary donations only.

Churchtown Parish Magazine

POPE DIES AGAIN

British newspaper, 1978

Thirty women moon worshippers met on a hill on Wednesday night to dance naked in an ancient pagan ritual, but called off the ceremony when 150 men turned up to watch.

Saskatoon Star

CHURCH NOTICEBOARD

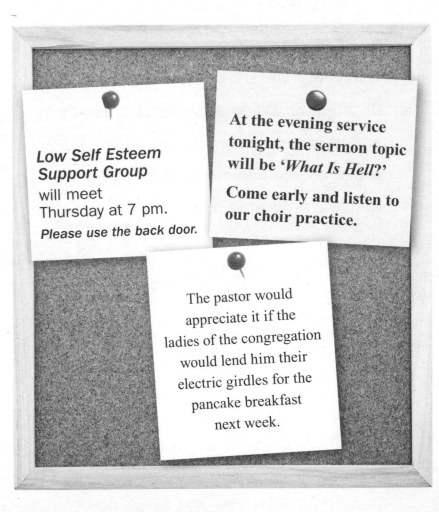

Low Self Esteem Support Group
will meet
Thursday at 7 pm.
Please use the back door.

At the evening service tonight, the sermon topic will be '*What Is Hell*?'

Come early and listen to our choir practice.

The pastor would appreciate it if the ladies of the congregation would lend him their electric girdles for the pancake breakfast next week.

R.E. HOMEWORK

Jacob had a brother called Seesaw.

Noah's wife was Joan of Arc.

The Pope lives in a Vaccuum.

If you marry two people you are
a pigamist, but morons are allowed
to do this.

S**ch**OOL
∧

exploded from school

ERROR: The Observer wishes to apologise for a typesetting error in our *Tots and Toddlers* advertising feature last week which led to Binswood Nursery School being described as serving 'children casserole' instead of chicken casserole.

Leamington Spa Observer

SCHOOL HOMEWORK BLOOPERS

Moths eat hardly anything but holes.

Herrings swim about
the sea in shawls.

Do you like my shawl?

The appendix is a part of a book for which
nobody has found much use.

Mrs Pearson said I could stay in
at playtime and help her sick up
some pictures on the wall.

Lowry's pictures were mostly
about the different prats
of Manchester.

'Morrissey'

L.S.Lowry

(Prats of Manchester)

The headteacher likes to snivel
around on a black chair in his
office.

If you are really naughty you get exploded from school.

Once there was a dog in the playground, and we went to smoke it but the dinner lady told us to keep away.

I helped my Dad in the garage. He let me hit some nails in with his hamster.

The pilot was bound to crash the plane. The moment he saw his wig come loose and fall to the ground he knew there was no chance of survival.

KID LOGIC

HOMEWORK BLOOPERS WHICH DISPLAY PROFOUND WISDOM

Faith is believing what you know to be untrue.

When a man is married to one woman it is called monotony.

Depth is height upside down.

A criminal is someone who gets caught.

Anatomy is something we all have but looks better on girls.

The future of 'I give' is 'You take'.

Poetry is when every line starts with a capital letter.

Diplomacy is saying the nasty things in the nicest ways.

EXAM VISUALS

Find x.

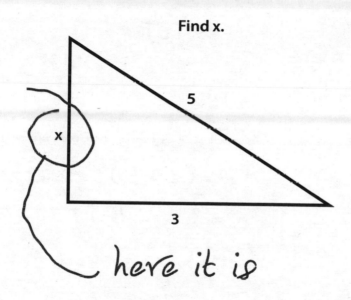

here it is

PETER

4c) Expand

$(a+b)^n$ Very Funny Peter.

$= (a + b)^n$

$= (a + b)^n$

$= (a + b)^n$

etc ...

2. A 3-kg object is released from rest at a height of 5m on a curved frictionless ramp. At the foot of the reamp is a spring of force constant k = 100 N/m. The object slides down the ramp and into the spring, compressing it at a distance x before coming to rest;

10   (a) Find x,

5   (b) Does the object continue to move after it comes to rest? If yes, how high will it go up the slope before it comes to rest?

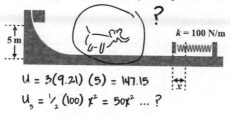

$k = 100$ N/m

$U = 3(9.21)(5) = 147.15$

$U_s = \frac{1}{2}(100)\, x^2 = 50 x^2 \ldots ?$

no. there is an <u>elephant</u> in the way.

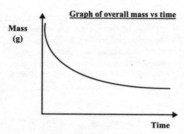

Graph of overall mass vs time

Mass
(g)

Time

1. Explain the shape of the graph.

Its curvy, with a higher bit at the end and a rather
aesthetically pleasing slope downwards to a pretty flat
strait bit. The actual graph itself consists of 2 strait
lines meeting at the left hand corner of the graph
and moving away at a 90 angle. Each line has an
arrow head on the end.

(d) How would you verify that the mutants identified by phenotype in your screen are true loss of *Jaw-D* mutations? (2 marks)

use the radioactive ooze!

TEENAGE
MUTANT
NINJA
TURTLES

I wish I could give you marks for this! LOVE IT!

Explain why phosporus trichloride (PCl$_3$) is polar.

God made it that way.

□⊏

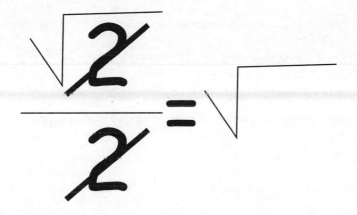

$$\frac{\sqrt{2}}{2} = \sqrt{}$$

signs & small Ads

STINKY

kennel for sale

DOG KENNEL, suit medium-sized dog. Good condition. Very turdy. Buyer collects. £9.99.

Wisbech Standard

Sign outside stable

THREE purple and gold stemmed goblin glasses, each with a different picture of Leaning Tower of Pizza. £10.

Ellesmere Port Pioneer

If you bought our course: *How to Fly Solo in Six Easy Lessons*, we apologize for any inconvenience caused by our failure to include the last chapter, titled: *How to Land Your Plane Safely*. Send us your name and address and we will send it to you post-haste.

Advert in World Magazine

Crash courses are available for
those wishing to learn to drive
very quickly.

Advert in Eastbourne Gazette

FOR SALE: 83 Ford Grandad.

Wolverhampton Express and Star

Applications for membership now being accepted for the Candlelight Room. A discreet Discotheque for the over 215's.

Northampton Evening Telegraph

FOR SALE:

antique desk suitable for
lady with thick legs and
large drawers.

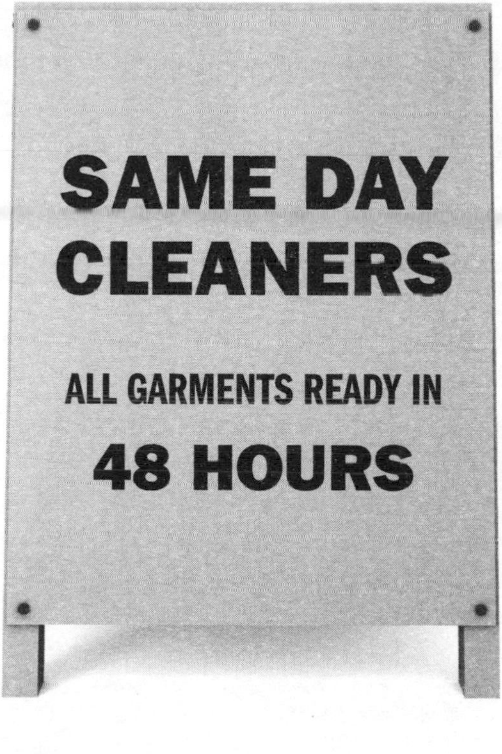
SAME DAY
CLEANERS
ALL GARMENTS READY IN
48 HOURS

TIRED of cleaning yourself? Let me do it for you.

We do not tear your clothes with machinery – we do it carefully by hand

Sign outside laundry

LADY, 65, reasonable looks, medium build, 65, likes short walks, outings, the occasional drunk.

Westmorland Gazette

DECORATOR Specializes in inferior work.

Immediate attention. Estimates free.

Hemel Hempstead Gazette

FORMER NAVY OFFICER now in business, late 30s, seeks sincere lady, late or early 20s. Ex-nuns or athletes given priority, any religion.

Irish Independent

1 GOLDEN LABRADOR Dog for sale,
2 years old, good driver, clean licence.

Hampshire paper

Waiting limited to
60 minutes
in any one hour

INFLATABLE RUBBER DINGHY FOR SALE
Good as new apart from slight puncture. £25

Sign in London department store

Sign outside dry cleaner in South Korea

**PUBLICIZE
YOUR BUSINESS
ABSOLUTELY FREE!**
Send $6

Now is your chance to have your ears pierced and get an extra pair to take home, too.

ILLITERATE?
Write today
for free help.

ONE MILLION PEOPLE IN AUSTRALIA CAN'T READ.

Are you one of them?

Entrepreneur Magazine

Save regularly in our bank.

You'll never reget it.

sports

OFFSIDE!

With seven minutes gone the packed terraces erupted as Butler struck the ball into Liverpool's net, but the linesman's fag was aloft indicating offside.

Observer

'Get on with it!' shouted the crowd, as half-back James paused with his foot on the ball. He did, and it produced a goat.

Sports news in Sunday paper

Spurs have similar ambitions, and are second, one point behind Bolton, after a 5-1 home win over Oldham Pathetic.

Evening News

Changes are likely to follow as the former England boss moves into the sea recently vacated by Ron Greenwood.

Daily Mirror

Paul Walker is doubtful with a toe injury while John Foster will have a late fitness test on his thing injury.

Hartlepool Mail

The announcement of the disqualification
was greeted by booze from spectators
at the pool.

Gloucestershire Echo

Perhaps 24 hours of speculation about Johann Cruyff's future affected the great man. Most of his dazzling runs ended with well-timed tickles.

Scottish Daily Record

The mystery fan behind the takeover bid for Port Vale today said he will pull out of the deal if his identity is revealed. It is understood Stone-based businessman Peter Jackson wants to remain anonymous until the contract is signed and sealed.

Staffordshire Sentinel

Liverpool's best chance ended when Beardsley shot himself.

Daily Express

Although a huge success, Eleni admits the marathon was no easy ride. She said: 'I was just getting over a virus and had to endure severe craps for about five miles.'

Galloway News

Hampshire elected to bath first on a pitch damp on top from the early morning rain.

Wolverhampton Express and Star

'Communist Olympics' Features Bomb Carrying and Grenade Throwing Events

Metro

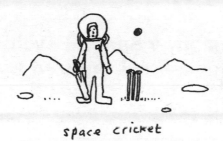

space cricket

India were without Kapil Dev, because of a bruised finger, a legacy of the first Test, and England omitted Chris Cowdrey and fielded three spacemen.

Brighton Evening Argos

Germany v Spain: Psychic Octopus Paul Unfazed By Death Threats, Says Keeper

Hey! It's the price of fame!

STAND IN: Former England rugby skipper Steve Smith replaces the injured Nigel Melville as scum half.

Daily Mirror

USA wins 1-1

New York Post

Goalkeeper celebrates promotion by spraying fire extinguisher in his pants.

Metro

BALLOON RACE:
Six Drop Out

Rugby star Rohei Yamanaka fails drugs test for trying to grow a mo

Metro

Simpore sisters axed from World Cup by Equatorial Guinea 'for being men'

Metro

During the Moscow Olympics of 1980 an athlete from Guinea Bissau refused to take part in the 3,000 metres steeplechase event. When asked why he would not run 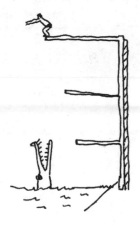 he explained that it was the water jump which worried him. You just don't jump into water in Guinea Bissau: there might be crocodiles.

From Steven Winkworth, Famous Sporting Fiascos

SPORTS WISDOM

Sir Bobby Robson

'The first 90 minutes are the
most important.'

Sir Bobby Robson

'There will be a game where somebody scores more than Brazil and that might be the game they lose.'

Sir Bobby Robson

'I would have given my right arm
to be a pianist.'

Sir Bobby Robson

'I am a firm believer that if you score one goal, the other team have to score two to win.'

Howard Wilkinson

'As with every young player, he's only 18.'

Sir Alex Ferguson, talking about a young David Beckham

kevin Keegan

'The 33- or 34-year-olds will be 36 or 37 by the time the next World Cup comes around, if they're not careful.'

Kevin Keegan

'I can count on the fingers of one hand ten games when we've caused our own downfall.'

Joe Kinnear

'I don't blame individuals –
I blame myself.'

Joe Royle

'Merseyside derbies usually last ninety minutes and I'm sure today's won't be any different.'

Trevor Brooking

We must have had 99 per cent of the game. It was the other three per cent that cost us the match.'

Ruud Gullit

'Don't tell those coming in now the result of the match. Now let's have another look at Italy's winning goal.'

David Coleman

'If you can't stand the heat
in the dressing room, get
out of the kitchen.'

Terry Venables

'If we score more goals than
they do, we will win.'

Kenny Dalglish

'That's the fastest time ever run – but it's not as fast as the world record.'

David Coleman

'I owe a lot to my parents,
especially my mother
and father.'

Greg Norman

'I was in a no-win situation, so I'm glad that I won rather than lost.'

Frank Bruno

'You guys, line up alphabetically by height.'

Bill Peterson, American football coach

T.V. Film and Theatre

you'll never walk
ALONE!

'You'll Never Walk Alone'
(Badgers and Hammerstein)

Lance A+ sports magazine

Marlon Brando is being paid £2,250,000 for 12 days' work in the new film, Superman. Believed to be the highest sum ever paid to a film star, Brando will also receive 11.3 per cent of the box office receipts, which should give him another £3.

Manchester Evening News

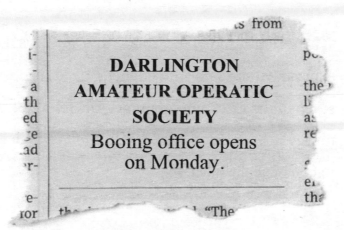

DARLINGTON AMATEUR OPERATIC SOCIETY
Booing office opens on Monday.

Darlington and Stockton Times

'The series, made in the Yorkshire Dales, was enormous fun,' said Christopher. 'I had made seven of the first 13 programmes when I broke my leg in a car crash, but I hop to be fit enough to complete the other six.'

Edinburgh Evening News

11.10

The Mayor of Casterbridge:
Repeat showing of the final part of 'Mayor of Casterbridge' – a threat in store for those who missed it on Sunday.

West Lancashire Evening Gazette

6.10pm: Pride and Prejudice

Mr. Bennett's estranged cousin, Mr Collins, writes to announce his imminent visit to Longbourne – the house he will inherit on Mr Bennett's death. Mrs Bennett rallies the residents to stop him setting up a minicab service.

Hampstead and Highgate Express

At the height of the gale, the harbourmaster radioed a coastguard on the spot and asked him to estimate the wind speed. He replied that he was sorry, but he didn't have a gauge. However, if it was any help, the wind had just blown his Land Rover off the cliff.

Aberdeen Evening Express

Further outlook:

Some rain,
becoming
milk later.

Yorkshire paper

ROAD CONDITIONS in the New
Forest were the worst known for years.
In several places the roads were lined
with cats unable to climb the
snow-covered hills.

Sussex paper

A depression will mope across Southern England.

Guardian

Fog and smog rolled over Los Angeles today, closing two airports and slowing snails to a traffic pace.

Los Angeles paper

HAVE YOU SPLOTTED
A BLOOPER?

If so, don't keep it to yourself
– Britain's favourite chameleon
wants to know!

Send your blooper to

bloopers@faber.co.uk

Don't forget to smell us where
and when you saw the blooper.

Better still, email us a photo or
scan. If we use it in the next
edition of Harry Hill's Bumper
Book of Bloopers we'll send you
a free copy, signed by Hairy.